JAPAN

THE SOUL OF A NATION

Photography by Michael Yamashita

Text by John Carroll

Published by Tuttle Publishing,
an imprint of Periplus Publishing

ISBN 0-8048-3436-9
LCCN 2002103669
Printed in Singapore

All photographs by Michael Yamashita except the following:
P. 6, Luca Tettoni Photography
P. 55, Luca Tettoni Photography/Brian Lovell

Distributors

Japan and Korea:
Tuttle Publishing, Yaekari Building, 3rd Floor,
5-4-12 Osaki, Shinagawa-ku, Tokyo 141 0032, Japan
Tel: (03) 5437 0171
Fax: (03) 5437 0755
e-mail: tuttle-sales@gol.com

Asia Pacific:
Berkeley Books Pte. Ltd.
130 Joo Seng Road, #06-01/03, Singapore 368357
Tel: (65) 6280 1330
Fax: (65) 6280 6290
e-mail: inquiries@periplus.com.sg

North America, Latin America and Europe:
Tuttle Publishing,
364 Innovation Drive, North Clarendon, VT 05759-9436
Tel: (802) 773 8930/(800) 526 2778
Fax: (802) 773 6993
e-mail: info@tuttlepublishing.com

Front Endpaper: The Miyako Odori (Cherry Blossom Dance) is performed by eight *maiko*, apprentice geisha, at the Gion Kobu-Kaburenjo Theater in Kyoto.
Right: A *hishaku*, bamboo ladle, sits on an ablution basin inset in a stone in the Ryoanji rock garden in Kyoto. Ritual cleanliness is a key characteristic of Japanese culture.
Opposite: Three geisha in exquisite kimono dance at a party in Kyoto's Gion entertainment district.

Photographer's Dedication
To Lil and Maggie

Photographer's Acknowledgements
Throughout my 30-year love affair with Japan, from my first "roots" trip in 1971 to my most recent assignment this year covering Tokyo Bay, there have been many people who have helped me along the way. Special thanks go to Nobuo Yabashi and the Yabashi family, my first employer in Japan; to Pacific Press Service president Robert Kirschenbaum, my close friend and advisor, as well as the entire PPS staff; to Kunio Kadowaki, my most frequent guide and assistant in Japan; to Shiro Nakane, who introduced me to the worlds of gardens and geisha; to National Geographic magazine and National Geographic Traveler magazine, on whose assignments many of these pictures were taken (with acknowledgements to National Geographic magazine for the photographs on p. 58 and p. 91); to Yoko Yoshioka, editor of JAFmate, who also sent me on many a Japan shoot; to Osama Iijima of Dai Nippon CDC and Nikon Cameras for their assignments in Tohoku; to Stan Braverman, former art director of Signature magazine, who gave me my first job as a professional photographer in Japan; and finally, thanks to my publisher, Eric Oey and his wife Christina, for their enthusiastic support.

CONTENTS

"The people whom we have met so far are the best who have as yet been discovered, and it seems to me that we shall never find among heathens another race to equal the Japanese. They are a people of very fine manners, good in general, not malicious. They are men of honor to a marvel, and prize honor above all else in the world. They are a poor people in general, but their poverty, whether among the gentry or those who are not so, is not considered a shame."

— Francis Xavier, *in his first letter from Japan to superiors in Goa*

The Japanese Enigma

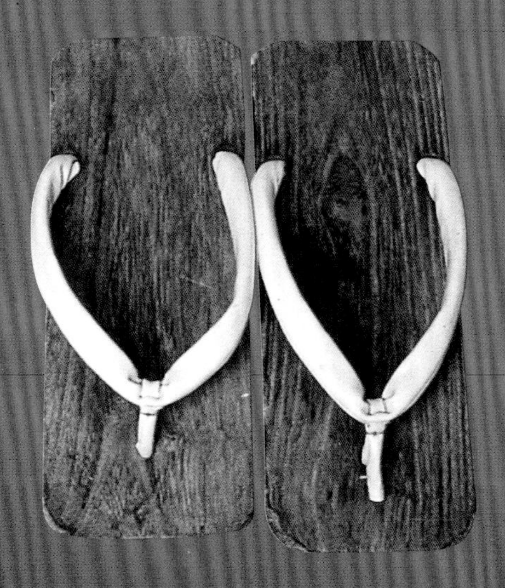

If Westerners consider Japan to be exotic, other Asians usually consider it an enigma. In fact, there is a question as to whether Japan should be classified as a sub-unit of the East Asian cultural sphere or treated as a separate civilization in its own right. Complicating the matter further, the Japanese frequently declare themselves to be unique, even while speaking of "we Asians" in contra-distinction to the West. But in the eyes of many Asians, Japan seems in Asia but not of Asia. What then is Japan?

The first key to understanding Japan and the Japanese is recognition of its geographical circumstances. The country lies some 160 kilometers off the Asian continent; it comprises four main islands (Honshu, Hokkaido, Kyushu and Shikoku) and over 1,000 small islands which, some 12,000 years ago, separated from the Asian mainland.

Climate, too, has been a critical factor in shaping the national character. Tokyo may be more southerly than Sicily but because of the workings of the monsoon system, Japan's climate can range from near tropical to sub-arctic, depending on location and season. The resulting diversity of scenery, flora and fauna is part of its attraction and never more so than in spring and autumn.

The origins of the Japanese still remain unclear. Despite the relentless mantra declaring ethnic and cultural homogeneity, it is likely that the Japanese are of mixed ancestry. What is clear is that the earliest inhabitants were physically different from those in the 5th century, when Japan finally established a centralized state during its Kofun (Burial Mound) Period.

We do not know whether the original inhabitants were replaced by, or intermixed with, latecomers. Nevertheless, DNA testing makes it clear that the Japanese of historical times belong to a genetic pool that covers the Korean peninsula, much of north China and Mongolia, possibly originating in the Lake Baikal area.

The basic design of Japanese homes, however – wooden frames with thin removable walls – suggests southern origins. Okinawan culture offers hints about what core Japanese culture might have been like since the local religion and creation myths are similar to those in Japan,

By around AD 400 the Yamato dynasty, which may have originated in Kyushu, established a central government of sorts on the Nara Plain. This was a period of huge tumulus building. The largest were reserved for the emperors whose power even

Previous page, left: A pair of wooden *geta*, slippers, at the venerable Tawaraya Inn, which has been operating for more than three centuries.
Previous page, right: Snow falls on the Nijubashi bridge of the Imperial Palace in Tokyo.
Left: The austere elegance of the Daibutsu-den hall of the Todaiji in Nara, the world's largest wooden building and home to the Great Buddha.
Right: A bird's-eye view of the imposing *Daibutsu*, Great Buddha, in Kamakura accentuates its weathered patina. Its asymmetrical proportions make the view from about five meters back the most impressive.

at this early stage seems to have been more symbolic and religious than political.

In 552 Buddhism was formally introduced. It marked a turning point in the archipelago's history, sparking a cultural revolution and forcing growth of a scale seldom seen in the world.

Just as the Greeks had generously borrowed elements of their civilization from Egypt and the Orient, the Japanese learned eagerly from China and Korea and, through them, from India. There followed the Taika Reform of 645 that attempted to transplant a system of strict centralized government modeled on that of Tang China. All agricultural land was declared the property of the Imperial House. The system never really worked yet the changes were still momentous.

In 710 construction began on the country's first permanent capital at Nara and the imposing 15 meter *Daibutsu,* Buddha, was built there a mere 40 years after advanced bronze-molding techniques had been introduced from the mainland.

The Heian period, named after the capital Heian-kyo, (today's Kyoto) followed from 794 to 1185 and was one of the high points of Japanese civilization.

It was also the most feminine of periods in history; the aristocrats, or "dwellers among clouds" as they were referred to, gave themselves up to the sophisticated pursuit of love. A potential beau would be judged on his calligraphy, poetry or choice of scent. The reputation of a court lady could be made or broken by her choice of kimono for a particular function. The characteristically Japanese atmosphere of delicacy, grace, refinement and aesthetic understatement was already established by the reverence for such qualities.

Around the middle of the 12th century Japanese history took a major turn. Although cultivable land had been expanding, the amount of taxable state land shrank, which led to the devolvement of power to feudal lords. Many of these drew support from local warriors, *bushi* or samurai (the latter derived from the word *saburai* or "to serve"), who had their own land holdings. The two most prominent warrior clans, both of which claimed Imperial descent and were widely dispersed throughout the country, were the Taira (Heike) and Minamoto (Genji). Soon after the court allowed the unruly samurai to get involved, the centuries-old ban on political violence was quickly abandoned and warriors from around the country flocked to the banners of

Opposite: School children on excursion amble beneath the giant, vermilion "floating torii" of Itsukushima Shrine, on Miyajima—one of Japan's "three supreme views."
Below: "The proud do not endure, they are like a dream on a spring night. The mighty fall at last, they are as dust before the wind."—*Heike Monogatari*
The shades of the vanquished Taira clan seem to flit among the night shadows of Itsukushima Shrine.

one of the two predominant clans, frequently switching allegiances for financial gain.

Under their leader, Kiyomori, the Taira had the advantage at first and in fact took over the court, marrying into the Imperial family so that Kiyomori's own grandson, aged two, became Emperor Antoku in 1180. However, the autocracy and arrogance of the Taira had already alienated much of the samurai class and with Kiyomori's death the following year all hell broke loose.

Hounded by rugged eastern warriors raised by a wily Minamoto survivor, Yorimoto, and his half-brother Yoshitsune, the Taira met their end in 1185 at the sea battle of Dannoura. Yoritomo then eliminated all potential rivals, and founded a *bakufu* ("tent government") at Kamakura, south of today's Tokyo.

This became the de facto government of Japan for the next 150 years. Yoritomo, however, soon died in a fall from his horse and relatives of his indomitable wife, Masako, of the Hojo clan (ironically of Taira blood) directed puppet shoguns – who in turn controlled the emperors.

Most of the Hojo regents proved to be highly capable, and if it were not for the cool courage of the young Tokimune, who was in charge during the two invasions by the Mongol armies of Genghis Khan in 1274 and 1281, Japan might have been just one more tally in the long list of Mongol conquests.

Left and right: During festivals in the Takachiho region of Miyazaki Prefecture in southeastern Kyushu, dancers reenact Shinto creation stories. Local residents claim that many of the mythological doings of the gods in the Plain of High Heaven actually took place in this area.

Above: Flowers bloom outside the Atomic Bomb Memorial Dome in Hiroshima. In the immediate aftermath of the A-bombing, it was feared that nothing would ever grow here again.

Above: Visiting school children seem oblivious to the significance of the Nagasaki Peace Statue in the city's Heiwa Koen, Peace Park.

Above, from left to right: Three Ages of the Japanese Woman—a girl from Matsushima, a bride wearing the elaborate kimono and headpiece for the Shinto ceremony, and an old woman in Nikko.
Opposite: The vast majority of Japanese consider themselves adherents of both Buddhism and Shinto. Here a priest of the Nichiren sect beats a drum at Myorenji, a temple famed for its 17th-century raked rock garden located in the Nishijin textile artisan district of Kyoto.

In the 1330s Emperor Go Daigo staged an Imperial Restoration that eliminated the Hojo but led to nearly a century of civil war. In the meantime another shogunate, led by the Ashikaga clan, established itself in Kyoto and exercised nominal control over the warrior class. From then until 1600 Japan was almost constantly torn by civil war.

This was the period of *gekokujo,* "the inferior deposing the superior," during which many a man of humble origin rose to the top by doing away with his lord. Brother slaughtered brother; son drove out father. Of the approximately 260 great feudal houses known before the Onin War (1467-1477) barely a dozen survived to see the dawn of the 17th century.

It was late in the 16th century that a trio of warlord giants appeared – Oda Nobunaga, Toyotomi Hideyoshi and Tokugawa Ieyasu – and with fire, sword and wile proceeded to unite the country, a land which, behind the curtain of political chaos and warfare, had been undergoing tremendous social, cultural and economic development. By the time Ieyasu won the mandate at Sekigahara in 1600, it could compete in terms of power with the Europeans and Chinese. Trade was flourishing nationwide and barter had largely been supplanted by the use of money.

The first westerners to appear on Japanese shores, were Portuguese traders around the year 1543. Missionaries soon followed and over the next few decades the ranks of Christian converts in Japan swelled to perhaps 300,000 people, before the Tokugawa authorities decided in earnest to root them out – partly for fear of foreign invasion. Christians were subjected to fiendish tortures, and those who refused to apostatize died under horrible conditions.

From the early 1600s until 1853, when Commodore Matthew C. Perry came knocking at Japan's door with his "black ships," the shogunate's seclusion policy kept foreigners out and Japanese in. Yet the *sankin-kotai* system that forced the feudal lords throughout the country to visit Edo helped integrate the nation's transportation network and develop the economy. During the Edo period (1600-1867) Japan achieved such a high degree of economic integration that the foundation was in place for its rapid modernization after the Meiji Restoration of 1868.

The young samurai from peripheral feudal domains who overthrew the Tokugawa shogunate, quickly shifted gears and pushed through an institutional and psychological revolution designed to make Japan strong, independent and respected throughout the world.

By the time Emperor Meiji died in 1912, Japan was a world power with an empire of its own. But the Meiji modernization process that had made possible impressive triumphs on battlefields and global markets also contained the seeds of destruction that were to bear bitter fruit at Pearl Harbor and Hiroshima.

Left: Bathing outdoors in *rotenburo*, natural hot springs, such as this one at the Takaragawa Onsen, is a hedonistic pleasure all can enjoy.
Right: Whether in the city or countryside, Japanese bathhouses have always been centers for community interaction. This one is at the Hoshi Onsen in Gumma Prefecture.

Above: Scenes from the Tawaraya Inn in Kyoto. Service at such a first-class, traditional *ryokan* is fit for royalty, and is designed to pamper all the senses while appealing to aesthetic sensibilities.

Above, clockwise from top left: Japanese love to eat, but denizens of Osaka are especially famed for their lusty appetites. In the Dotombori entertainment district, a chef at the Wadoka Fish Restaurant prepares a tasty treat. Diners slurp down *ramen* noodles, ubiquitous throughout the country. A couple enjoys a cup of java at a café in the trendy Daikanyama district of Tokyo. A dedicated staff is an absolute necessity for such an establishment as the Tawaraya Inn in Kyoto.
Overleaf: The semi-traditional garden of the Adachi Museum in Matsue City, Shimane Prefecture. This quiet town was for many years home to the famous writer Lafcadio Hearn, whose Japanese name was Koizumi Yakumo.

"In winter as in summer the people live on raw vegetables and go about barefooted....They are fond of liquor....In their worship, men of importance simply clap their hands, instead of kneeling or bowing. The people live long, some to one hundred and others to eighty or ninety years.

— Excerpt from the *Wei Zhi (History of the Kingdom of Wei)*
c. AD 297

Traditional Japan

It is fascinating how foreign travelers to Japan, whether from the Asian mainland or the West, have made surprisingly similar observations even though their visits have been separated by hundreds of years or even a millennium.

Much that is typically Japanese has survived the Meiji Restoration, rapid urbanization and the Occupation after World War II. Although General Douglas MacArthur and his band of reformers more or less forced the Japanese into accepting a very liberal constitution, at heart the country remained an authority-oriented, vertical society. Today's Japan is indeed democratic, just like it is indeed a free market economy, but always true to them in its own fashion, always true to them in its own way.

For the roots of Japanese traditions we need to look to Shinto, the indigenous faith of the Japanese. In some ways, Shinto is similar to the religion of the ancient Greeks and the antithesis of monotheistic religions such as Christianity and Islam. Like the gods of Olympus, the Japanese deities as portrayed in the *Kojiki* and *Nihon Shoki*, are a lusty, rambunctious lot. These 8th-century official

神苑拝観

chronicles, based on earlier historical records now lost, weave in myths from various sources to sanctify Imperial rule and claim an ancient heritage on a par with that of China. Both the Imperial clan and other major, ancient clans claimed descent from the gods and goddesses mentioned in the creation myths recounted in these histories.

A visit to the Treasure Museum at Meiji Shrine in Tokyo can be enlightening. It contains "portraits" of all the emperors in the "unbroken line" (many historians have doubts about this oft-made claim) dating back to Jimmu, whose traditional dates are 711-585BC. Whether Jimmu, or many of the others prior to the 5th century, ever even existed is highly doubtful. It does show us, however, how far back the national cult extends, and the fact that from the beginning Japan's emperors (on a few occasions a woman) were surrounded by a religious aura. The early separation of the ruler from actual political power is probably the greatest factor in making Japan's Imperial line the longest living monarchy on earth.

Shinto grew out of an animism that attributed special powers deserving of respect to certain natural objects and phenomena,

Previous page, left: A mendicant priest with begging bowl in Tokyo.
Previous page, right: Participants in this Shinto ceremony at Nikko wear a variety of traditional costumes denoting specific function and status.
Left: The gorgeous Heian Jingu was built in Kyoto in 1895 to mark the 1,100th anniversary of the founding of the city. It is a reduced-size replica of the Imperial Palace as it looked at its acme of prosperity. The Chinese-style bridge shown here is in the sprawling garden.
Right: Imperial court musicians perform eerie-sounding *gagaku* music in the precincts of the Meiji Shrine in Tokyo. This "fossil" music form originated in Central Asia and reached Japan via Tang China.

ancestral spirits or even living mortals such as heroes. These are called *kami* or "gods." It is similar to the Polynesian concept of *mana*. Even today you can hear superstars referred to as the "god of baseball" or the "god of management." Shinto has three main strands: worship of *ujigami* clan gods, shrine Shinto including the conducting of seasonal *matsuri* (festivals), and court Shinto including the *Niinamesai* (Festival of the First Fruits) and other rituals that must be performed personally by the Emperor.

Much confusion has arisen abroad about the role of Shinto in the lives of the Japanese. Prior to the Meiji Restoration, the native religion was largely non-institutionalized. However, in their eagerness to develop an ideology that would advance national cohesion and their goals of *fukoku kyohei*, "a rich country and strong military," the Meiji leaders grafted court Shinto and traditional reverence for the Emperor onto Prussian-style nationalism. In fact, in the early Meiji period, the government actively persecuted both Christians and Buddhists. Both the Meiji Shrine and Yasukuni Shrine (where the souls of all who died in war in the name of the Emperor are enshrined) are products of this government effort at mind control and are not part of the mainstream Shinto tradition.

Love of nature might be regarded as the basic impulse of Japanese sensitivity and the source of its aesthetics. At the same time, the Japanese do not seem enthralled with raw, primitive nature. They like their gardens highly-stylized or strait-jacketed.

Left: Pontocho and Gion in Kyoto remain perhaps the two most traditional entertainment districts in Japan. Here you can often see geisha or *maiko*, apprentice geisha, on their way to daytime dance and music lessons, or nighttime engagements.

What after all could be more un-natural than a *bonsai* plant, a tortured and distorted creation – foot-binding for Mother Nature.

Japanese continue to place great emphasis on the ceremonial, as anyone who has attended a marriage, school commencement ceremony or company entrance rite well knows. And although geomancy is not as important as in China, Shinto groundbreaking rites are *de rigueur*. In such ways, Shinto remains very much part of daily life.

Shinto places the greatest emphasis on purity: look at the stark simplicity of primitive shrine architecture such as in the Ise Grand Shrines. They have been reconstructed afresh every 20 years, without nails, since time immemorial. These shrine designs, with their distinctive *torii*, gateways and *chigi*, crossbeams, suggesting southern origins, are often hauntingly beautiful. Who could even imagine cruel, vindictive deities lurking in such precincts? Whereas Christianity abhors sin, and Buddhism those attachments that cause suffering, pollution is what is to be avoided at all costs in Shinto.

There are more than 100,000 Shinto shrines throughout the country where Japanese of all ages come together to communicate with their collective community of the present and the past. They also stage festivals that can be expressions of everything from simple joy to wanton rapture. The writer Yukio Mishima referred to the latter as "vulgar mating of humanity and eternity."

Right: Geisha are true artists; some indeed are National Living Treasures. Dedication and perseverance are mandatory for the geisha who will have to undertake many years of rigorous training in the performing arts before she can be recognized as a true professional.

Top and right: Scenes from the *Shibaraku*, a popular, classic tale of good overcoming evil, performed in the Kabukiza Theater, Tokyo. The *kabuki* was the theater of the masses during the Edo period, but today is mostly the province of aficionados and the curious.

Class and income distinctions naturally disappear during such revelry, and perhaps this democratic spirit carried over to the pleasure quarters of the Edo period, since the cut of one's kimono, one's *savoir-faire* and the size of one's purse mattered more than one's pedigree in the theaters and brothels. The geisha house is one of the few places where something of this traditional culture of play lingers on today.

Another Japanese tradition with a Shinto connection that very much survives today is the sport of sumo. Matches were formerly held at shrines, and the salt tossing and other formalities were considerably more time-consuming than they are in this age of televised bouts. Sumo was formerly connected with fertility rites, which is easy to understand seeing as how sumo wrestlers

resemble some of the plumper members of the Seven Deities of Good Fortune, such as Hotei (commonly known abroad as "the laughing Buddha.")

Basic knowledge of Confucianism probably reached Japan even before that of Buddhism. Although it naturally played a major role in the development of the early Japanese state, the Chinese philosophy of officialdom really came into its own under the Tokugawa shogunate, when the syncretic neo-Confucianism of the Song Dynasty came to be seen as the perfect ideology to protect the status quo class structure. At the same time and throughout their history, the Japanese consistently refused to accept the "Mandate of Heaven" tradition enunciated by Mencius that allowed the people to overthrow a ruler who had lost his right to rule

Above: Dating back to 1053, the Hoo-do (Phoenix Hall) of the Byodo-in Temple in Uji near Kyoto is the only surviving part of a retreat of the Fujiwara clan. It contains 52 original *bodhisattvas*, enlightened beings, carved by Jocho.

through immoral behavior. In fact, the Japanese aristocratic instinct wanted nothing to do with the more democratic inclinations of the Confucian tradition.

Unexpectedly, the cult of loyalty to one's rightful lord pushed by the shogunate helped spark the "native learning" intellectual revival that laid the ideological foundation for the restoration of Imperial rule. It also bred a strong sense of nationalism, with one ardent Confucian scholar declaring that if Confucius himself were to lead a foreign invasion, he would go personally to stop him.

Actually, this was a bastard form of Confucianism since it attached the highest loyalty to one's lord or master rather than to one's parents. *Kabuki* plays showing heroes sacrificing their parents or children for the sake of a superior would no doubt have seemed depraved and even bestial to contemporary Chinese. Their relative emphasis on filial piety is a fundamental difference between Japanese and Chinese societies in premodern times.

Samurai fathers tended to exercise more power over other family members than did those from other classes, and through the Civil Code of 1898 the Meiji government extended this warrior ethic to the general populace by giving the father sole control over everything from disposal of property to decisions

Left: The *Miyako Odori* dance recitals held each April in the Kyoto's Gion are a rite of spring timed to coincide with the cherry blossom.
Right: This intimidating *Noh* mask is from the Takachiho region of Kyushu. Local residents claim that this is where Ninigi-no-mikoto, grandson of the sun goddess Amaterasu, descended to earth.

Left and above: Two glimpses of the *Saijo* festival. This is a harvest festival dating back to the Edo period and is held, annually, in October in the eastern part of Ehime Prefecture on Shikoku. Men dressed in traditional costume carry more than 130 *danjiri,* festival floats, containing *kami,* deities, while womenfolk take part in other rites.

Above: Two wandering Buddhist priests of the *shugendo* sect of mountain asceticism seem to have transcended the world of illusion.
Opposite: Matsumoto Castle in Nagano Prefecture is here bathed in an other-worldly purple light. The six-storey black-and-white castle keep was built around the beginning of the 17th century and contains numerous displays of weapons and other artifacts.

on marriages and divorces. Just as the nation's citizenry was to be totally subservient to the Emperor (and by extension his representatives), every individual's future was subservient to the whim of the family patriarch.

That too changed with the Occupation, as the Japanese scuttled (with alacrity) the patriarchal legal privileges along with the formerly gross interference in private affairs by the State. This is a good example of what Ruth Benedict referred to as a Japanese penchant for the "expendability of damaged goods" – both material and ideological

The effects of Buddhism on the nation's culture are incalculable. For one thing, the Japanese could easily accept that faith's emphasis on the impermanence of all things, since it reflected both their environment and their basic view on life. Although the early philosophically-preoccupied sects including Shingon (which was similar to Tibetan Buddhism), and Tendai appealed to the upper classes, during the Kamakura period the Pure Land (devotees of the Bodhisattva Amida) and Nichiren sects spread throughout the land. It was a process much like that of the European Reformation.

Acceptance of the Buddhist concepts of karma and the evanescence of life did much to hone the Japanese aesthetic sense. *Mono no aware*, that is a resigned sensitivity to the "pathos of things," runs like a sadly beautiful skein through the history of Japanese literature from the early Manyoshu collection of poetry, through the *Genji Monogatari*, the *Heike Monogatari* and the *haiku* of Basho to the modern masters.

Thanks to Shinto, the Japanese are not a morose people; thanks to Buddhism, they are not a shallow people.

Above, clockwise from top left: Tradition lives on everywhere in Japan. A Shinto rite takes place at Nikko; the peerless White Egret Castle at Himeiji illustrates how the Japanese always try to combine beauty with functionality; passersby stop to say a prayer before a row of statues of *jizo*, a protector of children and travelers; and a large *torii*, entrance gate, frames a snowy scene at the Meiji Jingu in Tokyo.

Above, clockwise from top left: A red bridge contrasting against green mountains seems to offer magical entry into the beyond; white-clad festival participants carry a golden *omikoshi,* god platform; path to a local shrine in Tohoku flanked by lanterns; and *henro* pilgrims engaged in the 88-Kannon Temple Circuit on Shikoku

"Except for the horrible policemen who insist on being continental, the people—the common people, that is — do not run after unseemly costumes of the West. The young men wear round felt hats, occasionally coats and trousers, and semi-occasionally boots. All these are vile. In the more metropolitan towns men say Western dress is rather the rule than the exception. If this be so, I am disposed to conclude that the sins of their forefathers in making enterprising Jesuits into beefsteak have been visited on the Japanese in the shape of a partial obscuration of their artistic instincts. Yet the punishment seems rather too heavy for the offense."

— Rudyard Kipling, Letter (1898)

Modern Japan

Sometimes today's Japan reminds one of a marathon whirling dervish who is finally beginning to lose some juice. From 1945 until 1973, the Japanese economy grew at an unprecedented rate. Never, in the 6,000 recorded years of humanity, has such a large national economy performed similarly. It worked out to a phenomenal annual average growth rate of 10 per cent or more. Who could have predicted that in 1945?

When the war ended, Japan's cities resembled colossal funeral pyres, their wooden and paper houses gone up in flame, melted bottles poked out of the gray ash like emeralds. In the single fire bombing of the Tokyo-Yokohama area on March 10 of that year, approximately 100,000 people lost their lives, and at least as many more perished in the A-bombings of Hiroshima and Nagasaki that followed. Altogether 2.3 million Japanese soldiers and 600,000 Japanese civilians died in the homeland or overseas. The nation was on its knees and on the brink of mass starvation.

Things became even worse as the American-dominated Occupation under General Douglas MacArthur took over. Food was almost impossible to secure outside the black market. On top of this, 3.8 million military men had to be demobilized and around 6.5 million Japanese repatriated from the colonies and battlefronts. In the immediate post-war period survival was the name of the game, and the United States pumped billions of dollars into the economy, fearful that in their tribulations the Japanese might be tempted by the siren song of Communism.

If the Japanese had not been so preoccupied with simple survival, they might have suffered a collective nervous breakdown because of the rapidity with which changes to the old order occurred. On New Year's Day of 1946 the Emperor of Japan renounced his "divinity," effectively gutting the State Shinto ideology. Ever since the Meiji Restoration, this official ideology, centered on Emperor-worship, had been the glue that had held society together.

What replaced this now-discredited doctrine was a "psychology of hunger" and desire for redemption in the eyes of the international community that in a few short years was to propel Japan to the top of the global industrial ranks. The purging of 220,000 political, economic, government, social

Previous page, left: A loquacious robot shoots the breeze at Space World in Kitakyushu City.
Previous page, right: Inside a bustling terminal at the ultra-modern Osaka International Airport.
Left: An aerial view of a crowded part of Tokyo.
Right: Rush hour at a Tokyo station. During an average day, three million people are said to transit Shinjuku Station.

WESTIN

leaders also proved a boon, because it brought fresh blood and innovative thinking to the fore, while the fostering of trade unions changed the face of labor relations. The "no war" clause in the new Constitution also freed up capital that would have otherwise been spent on armaments.

The heating up of the Cold War brought Japan firmly into Free World camp and it benefited from a free trade-for-foreign policy support bargain. The economy took off with special procurement orders generated by the Korean War. As early as 1956 industrial production had reached pre-war levels. Another boost came from the 1960 Tokyo Olympics. Two years later, Japan's economic juggernaut had overtaken the United Kingdom, and in the 1980s it left the Soviet Union in the dust to become the second largest in the world.

One of the most important keys to this extraordinary record of accomplishment was the nation's industrial policy, a carry-over from and improvement on pre-war command-economy practices, under which bureaucrats decided on what areas of the economy would be fostered through massive subsidies and protectionism till Japanese industries could take on any rivals in the world. From 1954 to 1971 investment in new industrial facilities rose to as high as 36 percent of GNP. Except for the selective acceptance of capital and technology, the Japanese

Left: The twin towers of the Floating Garden Observatory in Osaka seem to be awaiting a space launching.
Right, top: Out for the night, a couple strolls through Osaka's Dotombori, a major entertainment district.
Right, bottom: This is Shinsaibashi, another Osaka entertainment district. In Japanese cities, you'll never walk (nor wait at a traffic light) alone.

Left: Panoramic perspective of Rainbow Bridge, the gateway to Tokyo Bay. Red-and-white Tokyo Tower looms off towards the far left.
Above: You'll find no "huddled masses" under this replica of the Statue of Liberty on Odaiba in Tokyo Bay.

sought to keep the presence of foreigners to a minimum. Japanese workers accepted low wages and poor living conditions not only because of their dedication to the national mission but also due to the allure of the three economic "sacred treasures", namely lifetime employment, seniority-based advancement and in-house unions.

The establishment of the Liberal-Democratic Party in November 1955 further stabilized the economy, because it effectively marginalized the left. Prior to that time, conservatives had been divided into smaller parties preoccupied with factional competition. Thus, the party formed as a group of disparate lobby interests continues to be just that until this day. As a result prime ministers are usually weak, and the country frequently appears to operate on auto pilot.

Japan roared through the 1960s and even though it tripped up a bit during the 1970s oil crises, it recovered so quickly that it came to be known as the "Teflon economy." By the start of the 1980s, Japan controlled roughly 10 percent of world trade and by the mid-1980s the Japanese were clearly pretty well-satisfied with their lot. The housing situation was getting better fast despite skyrocketing real estate prices. Furthermore, the nation continued to chalk up enormous trade surpluses, suffered from little real poverty, had a much admired basic education system, cutting-edge technologies, as well as the longest life expectancies in the world for both sexes.

Then in 1990 the bubble burst and the total value of Japan's assets plummeted by nearly one-half in just eight months. The long economic downturn that followed has sapped the nation's morale and led to significant changes.

Japanese no longer take a certain kind of pleasure in be referred to as workaholics; recent polls show their loyalty to their employers as among the lowest of any of the developed countries. But they have turned to the pursuit of leisure, since it provides an opportunity to escape *danchi,* housing projects, or other cramped living quarters.

During the mid-1970s Japan's birthrate dropped below the breakeven point needed to avoid population decline, and has been heading downward ever since. With the population graying faster than in any other developed country and the public debt reaching crisis proportions, the future for young Japanese wage earners looks bleak.

Opposite: The crowd parties at a baseball game at the Fukuoka Dome, the gold standard for the world in high-tech stadiums. In recent years, soccer has challenged baseball's perennial popularity among the younger set.
Below: Friendly rivals shake hands at a Senior Citizens Olympics held in Kyushu. Japanese of both sexes enjoy the longest average life expectancies in the world.

One thing is for sure, Japan is a highly urbanized society, with roughly three-quarters of its people living in its amoebae-like megacities. No matter what the time, day or night, you can find a convenience store or eatery open in Tokyo and the other major conurbations. But just when the visiting New Yorker or Londoner begins to suspect that things are pretty much like at home, he will see something that brings him up short. Perhaps it will be the sight of a middle-aged Japanese in suit and tie perusing with the greatest of pleasure a sado-masochistic comic book, or a motley crowd lined up outside a *pachinko,* pinball parlor.

One of the greatest changes of the post-war period is that Japan has become a motor culture par excellence. The scenic beauty of much of the exquisite countryside has been scarred by a seemingly uncontrollable desire to cover everything with concrete and cars. The RV (recreational vehicle) is the latest craze, even though they are often nearly as wide as the residential streets they try to navigate on.

The same Japanese who is so utterly polite in business can become appallingly rude or even recklessly dangerous in public situations such as when driving a motor vehicle on a crowded city street or riding a bicycle on a sidewalk. That's the price of progress.

Left: Japan is a land of high peaks — many of them volcanic. Steaming vents belch smoke from the flanks of 2,290-meter-high Mt. Asahidake in Hokkaido's Daisetsuzan National Park.
Right, top: Summer skiing is an attractive option in spacious Hokkaido.
Right, bottom: A noodle break during a snow festival is one of the little pleasures of life in the far north.

Above, clockwise from top left: Pachinko parlors, love hotels and pincer-perfect crab restaurants help make kitsch architecture an urban art form in today's Japan. Two tripping options – a family suits up at the Kitakyushu Space World and a boy goes virtual at the Galbo Virtual Reality Theme Park in Ichikawa City near Tokyo. Capsule hotels like the Green Plaza in Tokyo offer all the comforts of home in a squeeze.

Above, clockwise from top left: Street scenes in Tokyo: A couple about to cruise the Gaien-mae district, rocking out in Yoyogi Park on Sunday, artistic inspiration can take hold at anytime, and window shopping in the trendy Harajuku district.

"Do not ask for any short cut. In the final analysis Heaven has its own natural way of doing things, and in order to obtain rice, the proper procedure is to cultivate rice plants. In the cultivation of rice plants, too, there is a proper procedure involving the sowing of seeds. Remember that rice plants never produce rice plants, and rice seeds never produce rice seeds. First, the seeds must grow into plants and then the plants produce seeds. From the beginning of creation there has always been this endless process of transformation and transmigration."

— Ninomiya Sontoku (1787-1856), influential agrarian reformer

COUNTRY JAPAN

"Although Japan's gods might have descended from the Plain of High Heaven her people sprang from its soil" Until recent decades Japan, like its neighbors in East Asia, was predominately a nation of farmers. Although during the Edo period, Edo, Osaka and Kyoto grew to be large cities, the vast majority of Japanese were tillers of the land, whether they owned it or worked as tenant farmers.

There were quite a few marginal people living outside of this feudal class structure, including hereditary occupational outcasts and *hinin* (literally "non-humans;" including lovers who had attempted love suicide but survived), as well as nomadic mountain tribes known as *sanka,* the snake-worshiping *ebune,* sea gypsy fisherfolk, and seafarers of the Inland Sea (some of whom were born on and died on their boats), actors, religious mendicants and other vagabond drop-outs from general society, the descendants of transplanted Koreans and Chinese, and the enigmatic *kugutsu,* puppet people, whose origins are murky. In its zeal to establish the myth of Japanese racial and cultural homogeneity, the Meiji government forced these minority groups to settle down and then pretended that they

had never existed, so that Japanese today are largely unaware of these interesting heterodox traditions.

Japan is desperately land-poor. Whereas there are about 58 million people in Italy, which is a bit smaller than Japan, there are 127 million Japanese crammed into their chain of islands. But while arable land totals 31 percent in Italy, it is a mere 11 percent in Japan.

Marginal areas, such as the Tohoku region of northeastern Honshu, have always been highly subject to drought, typhoons, frigid weather and other whims of nature that led to horrendous famine. Many of the deaths could be attributed to transportation problems and the fragmented feudal administrative system in the country. An official report on the famine of 1783 reads: "The famine is so terrible that out of five hundred families in the village only thirty have remained; all the others have died. A dog is sold for as much as eight hundred yen, a mouse for as much as fifty yen. Corpses are eaten, and some have dispatched the dying and salted their flesh to preserve it as a last resort against starvation."

The typical Japanese diet of rice, miso soup, a main dish of fish or whatever, and pickles is actually a development of the

Previous page, left: Products of the good earth in the neighborhood of the Akaishi River in northern Honshu.
Previous page, right: Fuji-san looks down benevolently on a tea plantation in Shizuoka Prefecture
Left: Although unable to compete with foreign imports, Japanese rice farmers are determined to preserve their heritage.
Right: This example from the Ogimacho Gassho Village is typical of the types of traditional rural architecture preserved in the Shirakawa region.

modern industrial age and came about when staples, such as the soybean, were imported from the Japanese colony of Manchuria. In fact, prior to the early years of the 20th century, in many regions only the ruling class or the wealthy could afford to eat rice regularly.

With the opening up of Hokkaido after the Meiji Restoration, the landless poor often flocked to this last frontier. However, they soon discovered that they could not grow rice in such a cold climate. Stories recount how, when one of these pioneers was dying, the members of his family would put a few grains of rice into a bamboo tube and shake it to encourage him to dream of a satisfying meal and the *furusato,* ancestral home, in warmer climes.

Below: Hokkaido is the center for raising cattle and horses, including thoroughbred racehorses. **Opposite:** Life in the "Snow Country"—along the Japan Sea, in the Tohoku district of northern Honshu and Hokkaido—can be hard.

Even as a full-scale industrial revolution made rapid strides under state sponsorship, with huge urban centres springing up, the cycle or rural life continued and home industries carried on. Along the Japan Sea, Tohoku mountainous regions and the poorer areas of Kyushu and Shikoku, farmers and their families continued to eke out a living by planting rice. This would be supplemented by the growing of assorted crops and the raising of silkworms. Thanksgiving *matsuri,* festivals, also signaled the approach of the hard winter months. Residents of the "Snow Country," also known as *ura Nihon,* "the back of Japan", were often lashed by fierce storms which would bring meters-high snow after slamming into the Japan Alps, and cut off inhabitants for weeks at a time. However, eventually the growing disparities of wealth and the vagaries of rural income would combine to create great unrest.

Land reform was arguably the most revolutionary and long lasting achievement of the Occupation. Before the war, tenant farmers and poor peasants lived miserably unstable existences, constantly vulnerable to the callous demands of nature and the moneylender – although the government prevented outright starvation.

With one stroke of General MacArthur's pen all that changed, and Japan became a nation of owner-operators. An estimated four million farm families benefited and this paved the way for the economic and political stability of the new Japan. Anything in excess of 10,000 square meters was virtually expropriated from absentee landlords and redistributed to poor peasants and tenant farmers. That and mechanization led to a 50 percent surge in rice output.

In the immediate post-war era, Japan had been a hungry nation, but by the mid-1950s it was becoming food-affluent, paying for food imports with its fast burgeoning industrial exports. At this point, the majority of urban dwellers probably had originally hailed from the countryside, and they were willing to bear the burden of hefty agricultural subsidies and pork barrel construction projects to help out their country cousins. That was certainly true during the go-go economic growth era, although with the economy now mature and in fact on a no-growth treadmill for the last decade, this benign tolerance for such a vast income transfer from city to countryside, or rather to certain interests there, may not long go unchallenged.

The failure of electoral reapportionment to keep pace with the shift of population – one rural vote can equal four urban votes – has meant that political power in Japan is still much concentrated in the countryside. Nearly every major political figure in the country, including the bulk of prime ministers, has represented a rural constituency. The result has been fervid protectionism in the agricultural sector, endemic trade disputes and the notoriously high cost of living in Tokyo and the other cities. Expensive make-work construction projects are one reason why roughly one-tenth of Japan's labor force is concentrated in the construction sector, and the public debt situation has become so precarious.

Actually only about 10 percent of Japan's farmers are now engaged in full time farming. In off-seasons, members of farm families have long flocked to the cities to engage in *dekasegi*, pick-up labor. At such times, the Japanese countryside can appear to be strangely depopulated, with the elderly predominating,

belying Japan's position as one of the most densely populated nations in the world.

One cannot overstress the importance of *furusato* or the "green, green grass of home impulse" in the Japanese collective mentality. If you visit a *karaoke*, sing-along bar in a Japanese city, you are certain to hear many of the patrons singing songs with lyrics like: "Is that little brook still leaping there?"

Huge numbers of the city dwellers do go home twice a year – at New Year's and during the *Bon* summer festival of the dead, nominally a Buddhist tradition, when the souls of departed ancestors and family members are believed to return from the mountains. As the Japanese like to say: "There are none who do not know the way." At these times, motor traffic in and out of major urban areas comes to a virtual standstill.

Significantly *hotoke*, the Japanese word for a departed soul, is the same word used for the Buddha. Indeed Kunio Yanagida, trailblazer of folklore studies in Japan, concluded that the ultimate core of Japanese religious and psychological feeling is collective communion with these ancestral *kami*. In that sense, Japan truly is a "land of the gods" and this is where the soul of Japan is to be found.

Left, top: Arita in Saga Prefecture is one of the most important ceramic centers in Japan. Imaemon Imaizumi is a famous 13th generation potter as are many of the masters at the kilns of the southwest. They are descendants of Korean émigrés brought back as prizes of war during Hideyoshi's invasions in the 16th century.
Left, bottom: Imari, near the city of Karatsu, is another premier pottery center developed by Korean potters. Here a 17th generation potter, Nakazato Taruemon, is shown at work.
Right: Unnojoku, about 20 kilometers north of Karuizawa, is a mountain resort in Nagano Prefecture readily accessible by the *Shinkansen* train from Tokyo.

Above: Rural scenes from around the country: Despite the fact that rice has always been the grain of choice among the Japanese, in former times in most areas peasants could only eat it on special occasions, and otherwise had to make do with millet, barley, sweet potatoes and such.

Above: Although today's farmers continue to grow rice, many have found that hothouse, truck farming (top right) provides a better income. Below left, are the oyster beds in the Amakusa islands of Nagasaki Prefecture, one of the least developed areas of the country.

"Japan is like a mask with two faces, War and Peace – the Sword and the Tea-bowl."

— Bernard Leach, *A Potter in Japan, 1952-1954*

A Nation of Aesthetes

"There, during the 14th and 15th centuries, the *sumi-é* tradition was developed to new heights by masters like Josetsu, Shubun and Sessho". One of the great appeals of Japanese civilization is the nation's highly-honed aesthetic sense – direct yet subtle, beautiful yet sad, so often austere, autumnal and threadbare, but sometimes a riotous expression of unrestrained joie de vivre. This is seen in, among other things, the Japanese garden, ink paintings, the tea ceremony and ceramics. It also finds expression in everyday life; for example, in the careful way that gifts are wrapped; in exquisite handicrafts, and in minor arts of the past such as *inro*, seal cases and pillboxes, and *netsuké*, carved fasteners.

The aestheticism of the Japanese is certainly rooted in their approach to nature as influenced by Shinto, which dates back to earliest times. But an imported foreign influence has obviously had a major impact too. That is, of course, Zen Buddhism.

Zen is a decidedly down-to-earth approach to life that rejects the abstruse and abstract, and favors intuitions and feelings arising from the "is-ness" of things over conscious thought and reason. According to tradition, it was established as a school by Bodhidharma

(Daruma in Japanese) who is said to have been a prince from southern India who traveled to China and for nine years sat facing the wall of a cave performing *zazen* meditation. Zen appears to have reached Japanese shores only during the Kamakura period, but thereafter it had a tremendous impact.

Through many hours of silent meditation or other practices, the Zen disciple seeks to clear his mind of all extraneous thoughts, be released from the confining unreality of self and enter the realm of nothingness, where he can transcend all duality, bounds and limits, communicate freely with the entire universe and become one with the absolute.

To open the path to enlightenment, Zen masters would offer their disciples insoluble (through logic) *koan*, riddles, or engage in *mondo*, dialogues that frequently ended in "blows, laughter or totally meaningless replies." The goal was *satori*, conceived as moral, spiritual and intellectual emancipation. This amounts to a creative state in which the mind spontaneously attunes itself to the utmost level of fluidity and mobility.

From the Kamakura period, Zen philosophy changed the Japanese concept of what a garden should be. No longer simply a venue for pleasure, it became a gateway to the secrets of life and death. These gardens – often dry landscapes – are representational in the sense that through careful asymmetrical arrangement they can allude to the tangible and in abstraction can suggest moods of purity or tranquillity.

Zen had inspired the master ink painters of the Song Dynasty (960-1279), and after the Mongol conquest of China, several prominent Zen priests and artists fled to Japan. To paint with black ink on white paper demands that the artist eschew all hesitation, and strive for extreme simplicity and purity of line.

Noh drama too was deeply influenced by Zen thought in its emphasis on *yugen*, a quality of quiet, profound beauty verging on the occult, akin to the thrill you receive when you gaze at a full moon veiled by thin clouds. A fine *Noh* mask almost breathes this mysterious feeling.

That brings us to *cha-no-yu* or the tea ceremony. Tea connoisseurs in Japan spend incredible sums on tea utensils and clothes to participate in the cult so that, all-too-often, a ceremony becomes nothing more than a snobbish exercise in conspicuous consumption. Nevertheless, at heart *cha-no-yu* is a simple spiritual ceremony designed to cleanse the six senses of contamination and the four principles governing this ceremony are harmony, reverence, purity and tranquillity.

Previous page, left: Colorful Japanese paper umbrellas of Kyoto.
Previous page, right: The classic Japanese garden, such as this example at Tenryuji temple in Kyoto, is designed to invite contemplation.
Opposite: The art of the *bonsai* uses unnatural means to outdo nature.
Above: The Japanese have shown a phenomenal ability to exploit the small in everything from *bonsai* shrubs and *netsuke* ornaments, to transistors and semi-conductor chips.

Within a formal garden, a stepping stone path leads up to the tiny entrance way of the teahouse – the setting for a tea ceremony. The treasured tea utensils themselves, and the carefully prescribed procedures, are just as formal and precise.

Although tea had been introduced into Japan before the Kamakura period, it was originally used as a medicine and to stay awake for meditation. As in China, the tea ceremony began in monasteries and spread to general society, assuming its full form under the inspiration of the iconoclastic Juko (1422-1502). It also acquired addicts among the Ashikaga shoguns and later Nobunaga and Hideyoshi, and during this latter period attained its peak under Sen no Rikyu (1521-91), the son of a wealthy merchant from the cosmopolitan free port city of Sakai (now part of Osaka).

Many stories are told of Rikyu's fiery relationship with the despot Hideyoshi. In the end, Hideyoshi ordered Rikyu to commit *seppuku,* although to this day the reason remains unknown. The master held a final tea ceremony for his disciples and then after smashing his tea bowl into smithereens proceeded to disembowel himself.

Although most Japanese would claim to admire the subdued, refined taste generally referred to as *shibui* (literally meaning "astringent" like the taste of a lemon), during the Momoyama period of Hideyoshi, an alternative, rather gaudy exhibitionism

Left, top and bottom: Despite appearing to be the height of simplicity, swept sand and rock gardens like these demand excruciatingly conscientious care.
Right: The world-famous Ryoanji Garden in Kyoto. Finding *satori*, enlightenment, among the crowds here can be a tricky proposition.

Above, from left to right: Three different types of roof eaves—a temple, a spa and a castle. Even today Japanese architects like to incorporate traditional motifs into their designs.
Right: "Don't say splendorous *(kekko)* until you've seen Nikko," a common saying would have it. It's a matter of taste and one not shared by the more sober of visitors.

gained popularity – the later Tokugawa mausoleum complex at Nikko might be considered its ultimate example.

Zen appealed to the warrior class because of its commitment to direct action and lack of formal doctrine. But, as D.T. Suzuki pointed out, that very freedom means that it can be adopted to almost any philosophy. However, a highly-developed intuitive sense does not necessarily make a moral giant. The famous swordsman Miyamoto Musashi, for example, was both a Zen adept and consummate *sumi-é* artist, as well a serial killer.

The sword was said to be the soul of a warrior, and consequently in Japan swords have been treated with near religious awe. In fact the production of these involved solemn purification rites by the swordsmith and his helpers within a consecrated enclosure. The end product was often a work of art, and its owner was also expected to be pure.

In battle a true samurai would forget both the presence of death and thoughts of survival. He was said to have an immovable mind and would perform in a state of *mushin,* no-mind, or *munen,* no-thought, devoid of all ego consciousness, not to mention inhibitions.

Left: As shown here at the Shisendo Garden in Kyoto, Japanese gardens are so designed that the effect can be quite telescoped and differ according to the point from which it is viewed. Garden designers also cunningly exploit "borrowed views."
Right: The Kenrokuen garden in Kanazawa, Ishikawa Prefecture is famed throughout the land. More than a hectare in area, it contains thousands of trees and plants, plus streams, bridges and teahouses. During winter custom-made *yuki-zuri*, rope canopies, are used to protect the trees from snow damage.

Above: The Ritsurin Koen garden took more than a century to complete, and is an eye-pleasing combination of bridges, ponds, pathways and carefully tended foliage.

Above: The garden of the Adachi Museum in Matsue might be taken for an illusion, were it not for the multi-colored carp thrashing around in the pond.

Far left and left: Simplicity and purity are two values that can be discerned in nearly all facets of Japanese life and art. They are clearly visible here in these photos of wooden *geta* lined up outside the Tawaraya Inn in Kyoto. The use of *tatami* mats even today in many Western style homes and apartments is further evidence of these yearnings. Even when a home has carpeting or wooden floors, Japanese will usually wear slippers rather than shoes. There are also *tatami* areas in many restaurants and in even in public facilities like libraries.

Top, left and right: The famous heart-shaped garden of the *Saihoji* or *Kokedera* (Moss Temple) in Kyoto, which was designed by Muso Kokushi. The blend of green bamboo, moss and foliage has an almost primeval feel to it.
Below: A view from the cool interior of a room facing the center lake of Ritsurin Koen in Takamatsu City, Shikoku.

Above, clockwise from top left: *Yuki-zuri,* rope canopies, protect the 160-year-old pine trees at Kenrokuen Garden from the weight of the snow; artists flock to the Meiji Gardens in Tokyo at the time of the Iris Festival; Kenrokuen presents different faces depending on the season.
Overleaf: *Miyako Odori* of the Gion in Kyoto. Not all artistic expression in Japan is understated and restrained.

"A day when Fuji is not to be seen
Through cold mist and showers
That, too, is a delight."
— Basho (1644–1694)

The Soul of Japan

It is said that the first sight of Mt. Fuji is not to be forgotten in this life or the next. Some, in fact, have declared that the sacred mountain, or Fuji-san as it is invariably referred to with affection in Japan, is the very soul of Japan.

The nearly symmetric form and well-nigh perfect cone of the 3,776-meter-high volcano, highest of Japan's hundreds of volcanoes, rises austerely but with power and grace from a base often shrouded in cloud to appear like a snowy, protective specter hovering over the land. When it is tinged with a transparent intensity, and a red glow suffuses the wreath of clouds, one cannot help but imagine that Sun Goddess Amaterasu Omikami – supreme deity of the race and progenitor of the Imperial line – is present.

D. T. Suzuki, for one, believed that the presence of Mt. Fuji in the central part of Japan's main island has much to do with the Japanese love of nature, and that its aesthetic beauty awakens in them spiritually pure feelings. This is perhaps what Yasunari Kawabata meant when, in his acceptance speech for the Nobel Prize in Literature, he referred to the "deep gentleness of the Japanese spirit" at its finest.

So strong has the cult of Fuji been that during the Edo period worshippers would trek here in organized groups to make the climb, while those at home would construct mini Fuji-sans as ersatz objects of worship. Lafcadio Hearn, on the other hand, chose the flower of the mountain cherry tree "spreading its fragrance in the morning sun" as the locus for Japan's *kokoro* or soul.

Or maybe the Zen master Dogen was on the right trail when he said: "Enlightenment is the voice of the bamboo; radiance of heart in the peach blossom."

Yet at the same time Fuji-san projects an aura of danger and titanic potential energy. Although it last blew in 1707, a recent study showed that an eruption on the same scale could paralyze the greater Tokyo area and cause inestimable damage. On a clear winter's day its looming presence can be clearly seen off to the southwest of the capital.

And, as anyone who has climbed the mountain on a hot summer day can testify, up close the poetry turns to the harsh reality of a cinder-strewn garbage heap. No wonder there is the common saying, "He who climbs Fuji-san once is a wise man; he who climbs it twice is a fool."

Previous page, left: Dancer representing a ghoul performs with mask and fan at a festival of the Chusonji temple in Hiraizumi, Iwate Prefecture.
Previous page, right: An employee of the Tawaraya Inn bows to greet guests. Etiquette in Japan is expressed both with physical gestures and through the careful use of complicated honorific language.
Left: Snow-clad Mt. Fuji towers over Lake Ashinoko and its "pirates" and weekend boaters. The lake is one of the prime attractions of the sprawling Hakone-Fuji-Five Lakes scenic recreation zone.
Right: A pagoda in a nearby town seems to be paying homage to the sacred mountain.

Above: A practitioner of *kyudo* or Japanese archery. The chief aim of this training is spiritual discipline, although in early medieval times the bow was the principal weapon of samurai, who were largely mounted.
Opposite: *Yabusame* or horseback archery is still practiced in Kamakura, Kyoto and a few other spots. Hitting a target while galloping at full speed in front of a crowd is no mean feat.

In all of these ways, Fuji-san might be considered as a metaphor for Japan, a land of contradictions and multiple meanings. In fact one of the characteristics of the Japanese genius throughout the ages has been the ability to accept innovations without abandoning what has gone before. Thus, for example nearly all the schools of Buddhism introduced into Japan during different eras continue to coexist today. And in the *ryobu Shinto*, dual Shinto synthesis, native gods became manifestations of Buddhas, or vice versa. The marvelous Japanese talent for assimilation frequently combines the seemingly unrelated to form a new harmonious, indissoluble unity, which in its turn will be preserved.

What then sets the Japanese apart from other cultures? If you visit a large bookstore in Japan, you can often find a whole section devoted to *Nipponjin-ron* tomes, in other words books that proclaim the "unique individuality of the Japanese race." Exponents generally point to the Emperor system and its supposed divine origins. At the same time, the origins of the Japanese people fuel a never-ending debate.

A recent prime minister of Japan raised hackles in many quarters when he referred to Japan as "the land of the gods." This was language that came straight out of the ideology of the pre-war militarist period, during which Japan was lauded as a peerless spiritual body uniting the Emperor, gods, ancestors and descendants. But what makes this statement particularly interesting is that it seems to infer that all other peoples are descendents of something else. All of which might be amusing, except that it affects how the Japanese think of themselves and treat others.

The Japanese word *kokoro* is variously defined as mind, spirit, mentality, heart, emotional sense, courage, resolve, affection, sincerity, sentiment and "the heart of things." In other words, what it really amounts to is that of being Japanese. In trying to consider what constitutes this Japanese "soul," we first must consider the natural environment in which Japanese civilization has developed. At least during the historical period, secure in their nearly impregnable island fastness, the Japanese were able to pick and choose what they wanted to adopt from abroad. Although until the Meiji Restoration the average person did not think in terms of being part of the nation Nippon, he or she definitely thought in terms of "us" and "them." Personal ties were based on proximity, and therefore foreigners were definitely beyond the pale.

友人会

Left: A group of *sumotori* lined up on the edge of the *dohyo* during a tournament in Osaka. Sumo is not only a time-honored ritual with arcane customs of religious significance, but also a highly popular sport with results appearing on the front pages of sports tabloids.
Above: The pre-bout rites, including tossing salt for purification, usually last longer than the actual bout. But the brief action can be mesmerizingly intense.

This is the basis of their *shimaguni konjo* island mentality and rampant "groupism." The fact that the Japanese people have never been dominated by any single, absolute religious faith and blithely worship numerous gods at the same time means that they reject, or rather do not usually think in terms of, any absolute, eternal truth. As Nikos Kazantzakis put it: "A Japanese has no need of metaphysical systems; he listens to the unmistakable voice of his heart – his race – and plans every one of his actions accordingly. This almost bodily certainty makes the actions of the Japanese simple, rapid, sure."

The Japanese have perfected moral relativism to a fine art. When those around them have reached a consensus that something is right for a given time, most accept it without demur – even if they actually think it is wrong. Of course, what is agreed upon as being right may quickly change according to circumstances. Critics would go so far as to say the Japanese lack a conscience outside the collective. When forced to make a judgement call, they will more often rely on their *kokoro* or *kimochi* (frame of mind) than rigorous reasoning. "Don't talk logic!" is a definite putdown in Japanese.

Among the many ramifications of this groupism is an emphasis on *wa,* harmony, that manifests itself in deference to

Left: A mounted archer in medieval equipage takes aim in Nikko. The horse has held an important place in Japanese history, and some scholars believe that the Japanese, or at least the ruling class in early historic times, were horsemen from the Asian mainland.
Opposite: Draft horse racing in Hokkaido. There are racetracks and off-track betting centers in most major urban areas. Many Japanese also enjoy horsemeat, known euphemistically as *sakura no niku* (literally "cherry meat").

authority, fairly amicable labor-management relations and a bottom-up management style. Traditionally, education and socialization taught a Japanese to sacrifice himself to the group in order to receive his true self. But the *hara gei* unspoken style of communications that gives Japanese such sensitive social antenna within a known context, works less well when they are dealing with outsiders.

Absolute identification can result in prodigies of mutual self-sacrifice on behalf of the group, whether in the singing of company songs or the working of inordinately long hours. Japanese salarymen march off to the office in the morning with company pins on their lapels, like samurai of yore flying their feudal pennants. This is taken as evidence of the much-prized virtue of *gaman,* that is perseverance or self-denial. Sometimes, however, this spirit of self-sacrifice can be taken to morbid excess and perhaps reflect a cultural soul-sickness, a case of the moth yearning for the flame, whether it be a kamikaze volunteer or a company warrior who literally works himself to death.

Giri, the peculiar sense of honor, duty or obligation that makes Japanese society so cohesive, is also more often directed towards the group rather than an individual. This ties in with the belief that the individual is duty-bound to avoid doing anything that would shame the group. Thus, when a company or other organization is caught doing something illicit, the top man will often resign to take responsibility – some even commit suicide.

Another manifestation of the compulsive need to follow the group lead is conformity, whether in fashion or mindset. That only reinforces the considerable influence of the mass media.

Above, clockwise from top left: Various forms of relaxation—a young woman practices the tea ceremony at Yabunouchi Tea School in Kyoto; guests at the Manza Onsen Hotel savoring a variety of dishes, some served in bento boxes; two revelers enjoying their sake in the bath; and purifying the hands prior to engaging in the tea ceremony.
Opposite, top: Denizens of the Unzen Jigoku (Hell) Spa in the Shimabara district of Nagasaki seem to be arriving on a bridge from Hades.
Opposite, bottom: Being buried alive in hot sand with the aid of shovel-wielding, female experts is a prized pleasure on Surigahama Beach in Ibusuki, Kyushu. A local hotel also boasts of its huge Jungle Bath replete with tropical vegetation.

Conversely, non-conformist, individualistic Japanese can be some of the most fascinating people in the world.

Throughout their history the Japanese have placed great emphasis on *mibun*, social status. That explains the tremendous importance placed on the exchange of *meishi*, name cards, within Japanese business circles. All too often a person is judged by his position rather than his personal qualities. This is ironic because in many organizations lower ranking managers are the ones who make the key decisions, and the top person is nothing more than an *omikoshi* to be presented to the public.

Conservatives in the country frequently complain that postwar Japan has lost its *kokoro*, and they blame it on everything from the Americanized educational system to unrestrained materialism. They demand that *Kimigayo*, the national song in praise of the Emperor, be sung in the schools and ethics taught in the classroom. This sentiment was expressed in outrageous fashion when novelist Yukio Mishima unsuccessfully tried to arouse the Self-Defense Forces in a *coup d'état* on November 25, 1970. Speaking to a crowd of soldiers from a balcony before committing *seppuku* he bellowed: "I thought the Self-Defense Forces were the last hope of Nippon, the last stronghold of the Japanese soul. But the Japanese people today think only of money, just money. Where is our national spirit today?"

With the continuing economic downturn, many observers are already saying that Japan's glory days are gone and that its economy is certain to be surpassed by China. But resilience is perhaps the prime virtue of the Japanese people. Time after time the Japanese have come back from natural disaster and manmade misfortune to thrive and flourish. They may well do so again.

Selected Further Reading

Previous page: Revelers enjoy an alcohol-fueled *hanami*, a flower-viewing party, beneath cherry blossoms of Hitsujiyama Park in Chichibu City, Saitama Prefecture. This is a centuries-old nationwide custom. Sometimes the tipplers can get pretty wild, as is demonstrated yearly in Ueno Park in Tokyo.
Above: Back to nature with a vengeance at the Takaragawa Onsen.
Overleaf: An aerial view of the West Shinjuku sub-city center in Tokyo.

A Japanese Mirror: Heroes and Villains of Japanese Culture, Ian Buruma, Penguin, 1988

The Anatomy of Dependence, Takeo Doi, Kodansha International, 2002

The Chrysanthemum and the Sword: Patterns of Japanese Culture, Ruth Benedict, Charles E. Tuttle Company, Inc., 1954

The Enigma of Japanese Power, Karel van Wolferen, Vintage Books, 1990

The Floating World in Japanese Fiction, Howard Hibbett, Tuttle Publishing, 2001

In Praise of Shadows, Junichiro Tanizaki, Leete's Island Books, 1988

Japan: A Short Cultural History, George B. Sansom, Charles E. Tuttle Company, Inc., 1973

Japan As Number One: Lessons for America, Ezra Vogel, Universe.com, 1999

Japan: The Story of a Nation, Edwin O. Reischauer, Charles E. Tuttle Company, Inc., 1981

Japan, The System that Soured: The Rise and Fall of the Japanese Economic Miracle, Richard Katz, M.E. Sharpe, 1988

The Japanese Today: Change and Continuity, Edwin O. Reischauer and Marius Jansen, Harvard University Press, 1995

The Nobility of Failure, Ivan Morris, Noonday Books, 1988

The Roads to Sata: A 2,000 Mile Walk Through Japan, Alan Booth, Kodansha International, 1997

Zen and Japanese Culture, D.T. Suzuki, Princeton University Press, 1970